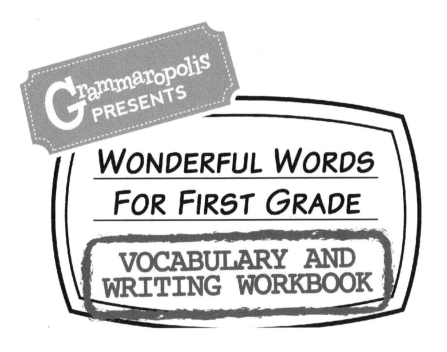

Grammaropolis PRESENTS

WONDERFUL WORDS
FOR FIRST GRADE

VOCABULARY AND WRITING WORKBOOK

BY ORDER OF

The Mayor of Grammaropolis

Written by Christopher Knight
Interior Design by Christopher Knight
Cover Design by Mckee Frazior
Grammaropolis Character Design by Powerhouse Animation & Mckee Frazior

ISBN: 9781644420690
Copyright © 2021 by Grammaropolis LLC
All rights reserved.
Published by Six Foot Press
Printed in the U.S.A.

Grammaropolis.com
SixFootPress.com

Grammaropolis PRESENTS

WONDERFUL WORDS
FOR FIRST GRADE

VOCABULARY AND
WRITING WORKBOOK

GRAMMAROPOLIS BOOKS

HOUSTON

FROM THE DESK OF THE MAYOR

Greetings, fellow wordsmith!

Thank you so much for using this workbook. I hope you have fun learning some new vocabulary words!

As you know, many words can act as multiple parts of speech; it all depends on how they're used in the sentence. For the sake of clarity and simplicity (and because we didn't have enough space on the page!), the definitions in this workbook include only one part of speech for each word.

It's great to know a lot of vocabulary words, but the real reason we expand our vocabulary is so that we can communicate more effectively. That's why I've added a writing exercise, with optional prompts, at the end of each section.

Thanks again for visiting Grammaropolis. I hope you enjoy your stay!

—The Mayor

TABLE OF CONTENTS

How to Use the Vocabulary Pages 6

Parts of Speech Review 7

Section One   9

Section One Word Review 18

Story One 19

Section Two   23

Section Two Word Review 32

Story Two 33

Section Three   37

Section Three Word Review 46

Story Three 47

Section Four   51

Section Four Word Review 60

Story Four 61

Section Five   65

Section Five Word Review 74

Story Five 75

Section Six   79

Section Six Word Review 88

Story Six 89

Index of Words Used 94

How to Use The Vocabulary Pages

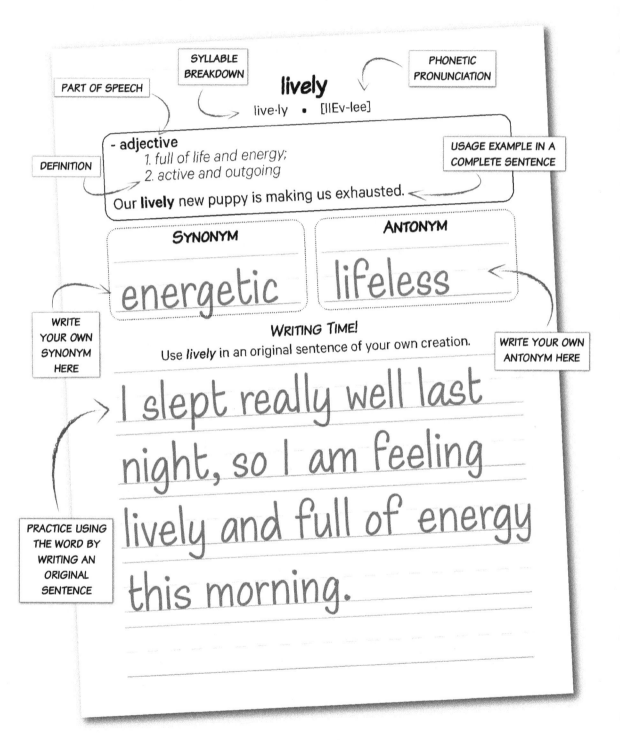

PART OF SPEECH

SYLLABLE BREAKDOWN

PHONETIC PRONUNCIATION

lively

live·ly • [llEv-lee]

DEFINITION

- adjective
1. full of life and energy;
2. active and outgoing

USAGE EXAMPLE IN A COMPLETE SENTENCE

Our **lively** new puppy is making us exhausted.

SYNONYM

ANTONYM

energetic

lifeless

WRITE YOUR OWN SYNONYM HERE

WRITE YOUR OWN ANTONYM HERE

Writing Time!
Use *lively* in an original sentence of your own creation.

I slept really well last night, so I am feeling lively and full of energy this morning.

PRACTICE USING THE WORD BY WRITING AN ORIGINAL SENTENCE

Important Note: Synonyms and antonyms for nouns might be harder to come up with than they are for verbs and adjectives, but do your best!

THE PARTS OF SPEECH REVIEW

Every word acts as at least one of the eight parts of speech. In this workbook, you'll find nouns, verbs, and adjectives. Here are some things you need to remember about them!

NOUNS
A noun can name a person, place, thing, or idea.

Naming a person:
Jason is my very best **friend**.

Naming a place:
Becks Prime is my favorite **restaurant**.

Naming a thing:
That **ball** is my favorite **toy**.

Naming an idea:
Honesty and **loyalty** are my best **qualities**.

VERBS
An action verb expresses mental or physical action, and a linking verb expresses a state of being.

Expressing physical action:
Richard **jumped** across the river.

Expressing mental action:
Richard **considered** jumping across the river.

Expressing a state of being:
Richard **feels** bad. He **is** sorry for jumping across the river.

ADJECTIVES
*An adjective modifies a noun or a pronoun and tells **what kind, which one, how much,** or **how many**.*

Modifying a noun:
The **quick brown** fox jumped over the **enormous red** fence at the **first** sign of trouble.

Modifying a pronoun:
They are **satisfied** with the answer, but I am still **curious**.

There are five other parts of speech you won't find in this workbook, but that doesn't mean they're not important!

ADVERBS
*An adverb modifies a verb, an adjective, or another adverb and tells **how, where, when,** or **to what extent**.*

PRONOUNS
A pronoun takes the place of one or more nouns or pronouns.

CONJUNCTIONS
A conjunction joins words or word groups.

PREPOSITIONS
A preposition shows a logical relationship or locates an object in time or space.

INTERJECTIONS
An interjection expresses strong or mild emotion.

SECTION ONE: WORD PREVIEW
Welcome to your eight new favorite words!

When you encounter a new word, take a moment to consider what it might mean.

1. Think about the word and circle what part of speech you think it is. *(Many words can act as more than one part of speech, depending on how they're used in the sentence, **so only choose one part of speech below**.)*

2. Come up with a brief definition of the word in the part of speech you've chosen. It doesn't have to be the *correct* definition—just do your best.

basket
Part of Speech: noun   verb   adjective

*Definition:*_____

_____

chat
Part of Speech: noun   verb   adjective

*Definition:*_____

_____

crash
Part of Speech: noun   verb   adjective

*Definition:*_____

_____

ignore
Part of Speech: noun   verb   adjective

*Definition:*_____

_____

bundle
Part of Speech: noun   verb   adjective

*Definition:*_____

_____

nibble
Part of Speech: noun   verb   adjective

*Definition:*_____

_____

alone
Part of Speech: noun   verb   adjective

*Definition:*_____

_____

narrow
Part of Speech: noun   verb   adjective

*Definition:*_____

_____

basket

bas·ket • [bAs-kit]

- noun

1. a receptacle made of interwoven material

We took our lunch to the park in a picnic **basket**.

SYNONYM	ANTONYM

WRITING TIME!

Use *basket* in an original sentence of your own creation.

chat

chat • [chAt]

- verb

1. to talk in a light and familiar manner

Jason and Frankie had a brief **chat** before they went to class.

SYNONYM	ANTONYM

WRITING TIME!

Use *chat* in an original sentence of your own creation.

crash

crash • [krAsh]

- verb

  1. to break into pieces violently and noisily;
  2. to enter or attend without invitation or credentials

  The glass **crashed** to the ground with a loud noise.

SYNONYM	ANTONYM
_____	_____
_____	_____

WRITING TIME!
Use *crash* in an original sentence of your own creation.

_____

_____

_____

_____

_____

_____

_____

_____

_____

ignore

ig·nore • [ig-nOR]

- verb
  1. to refuse to take notice of

I tried to get Julia's attention, but she **ignored** me!

SYNONYM	ANTONYM

WRITING TIME!

Use *ignore* in an original sentence of your own creation.

bundle

bun·dle • [bUHn-duhl]

- **noun**

1. *a number of things fastened together into a loose package*

Hank grabbed **bundle** of pens and pencils and ran away.

SYNONYM	ANTONYM
_____	_____
_____	_____

WRITING TIME!
Use *bundle* in an original sentence of your own creation.

_____

_____
_____

_____

_____
_____

_____

_____
_____

nibble

nib·ble • [nIb-uhl]

- **verb**
  1. *to bite lightly or gently;*
  2. *to eat in small bits*

I wasn't very hungry, so I just **nibbled** on my sandwich.

SYNONYM

ANTONYM

WRITING TIME!

Use *nibble* in an original sentence of your own creation.

alone

a·lone • [uh-lOHn]

> **- adjective**
>   *1. separated, especially physically: isolated;*
>
> Do you like being **alone**, or do you prefer being with other people?

SYNONYM	ANTONYM
_____	_____
_____	_____

WRITING TIME!

Use *alone* in an original sentence of your own creation.

_____

_____

_____

_____

_____

_____

_____

_____

_____

_____

narrow

nar·row • [nAIR-oh]

- adjective

1. of little breadth, especially in comparison with length

The wide table almost didn't fit through the **narrow** doorway.

SYNONYM	ANTONYM

WRITING TIME!

Use *narrow* in an original sentence of your own creation.

_____

_____

_____

_____

_____

_____

_____

_____

_____

Section One: Word Review

Congratulations on learning eight amazing new words! Remember that the whole point of learning new vocabulary is actually to use it, so let's put your new vocabulary to use.

1. Review the words you've learned. Consider what ideas come to mind when you say the words. How about when you read the definitions?
2. Circle at least **two** of your favorites. You'll get to use these when you write your very own story!

basket ——— noun

1. *a receptacle made of interwoven material*

chat ——— verb

1. *to talk in a light and familiar manner*

crash ——— verb

1. *to break into pieces violently and noisily;*
2. *to enter or attend without invitation or credentials*

ignore ——— verb

1. *to refuse to take notice of*

bundle ——— noun

1. *a number of things fastened together into a loose package*

nibble ——— verb

1. *to bite lightly or gently;*
2. *to eat in small bits*

alone ——— adjective

1. *separated, especially physically: isolated*

narrow ——— adjective

1. *of little breadth, especially in comparison with length*

STORY ONE

1. List the words you've chosen:

_____

2. Write a story that incorporates all of your chosen words. If you can't think of anything to write about, consider these suggestions:
   - Write a story about a rock that can talk.
   - Write a story that takes place in the middle of a snowstorm.

_____

_____
_____

_____
_____

_____
_____

_____
_____

_____
_____

Wonderful Words for First Grade Vocabulary & Writing Workbook ©2021 Grammaropolis LLC

SECTION TWO: WORD PREVIEW
Welcome to your eight new favorite words!

When you encounter a new word, take a moment to consider what it might mean.

1. Think about the word and circle what part of speech you think it is. *(Many words can act as more than one part of speech, depending on how they're used in the sentence, **so only choose one part of speech below**.)*

2. Come up with a brief definition of the word in the part of speech you've chosen. It doesn't have to be the *correct* definition—just do your best.

focus
Part of Speech: noun   verb   adjective

Definition:_____

trust
Part of Speech: noun   verb   adjective

Definition:_____

repeat
Part of Speech: noun   verb   adjective

Definition:_____

creak
Part of Speech: noun   verb   adjective

Definition:_____

bolt
Part of Speech: noun   verb   adjective

Definition:_____

wicked
Part of Speech: noun   verb   adjective

Definition:_____

costume
Part of Speech: noun   verb   adjective

Definition:_____

misty
Part of Speech: noun   verb   adjective

Definition:_____

focus

fo·cus • [fOH-kuhs]

- verb
1. to pay particular attention to;
2. to adjust the focus of (as the eye or a lens)

Let's **focus** on what's really important: chocolate.

SYNONYM	ANTONYM

WRITING TIME!

Use *focus* in an original sentence of your own creation.

trust

trust • [trUHst]

- verb
    1. to place confidence in : depend;
    2. to rely on the truthfulness or accuracy of

He **trusts** me because I always tell the truth.

SYNONYM	ANTONYM

WRITING TIME!
Use *trust* in an original sentence of your own creation.

repeat

re·peat • [ri-pEEt]

> **- verb**
> 1. *to say or state again;*
> 2. *to make, do, or perform again*
>
> Please **repeat** that because I didn't hear you the first time.

SYNONYM	ANTONYM

WRITING TIME!
Use *repeat* in an original sentence of your own creation.

creak

creak • [krEEk]

- verb

1. to make a prolonged grating or squeaking sound

The rusted hinges **creaked** loudly when the door closed.

SYNONYM	ANTONYM

WRITING TIME!

Use *creak* in an original sentence of your own creation.

bolt

bolt • [bOHlt]

> **- verb**
>   *1. to move suddenly (as from surprise or fright);*
>   *2. to move rapidly*
>
> My cat **bolted** out of the room when I dropped the plate.

SYNONYM	ANTONYM

WRITING TIME!
Use *bolt* in an original sentence of your own creation.

wicked

wick·ed • [wIk-uhd]

- **adjective**

    1. evil in character, behavior, tendency, or influence

A good fairy tale needs a **wicked** villain to root against.

Synonym

Antonym

Writing Time!
Use *wicked* in an original sentence of your own creation.

costume

cos·tume • [kOH-stoom]

- noun

> 1. a set of clothes in a style typical of a particular country, occupation, occasion, or historical period

I wore a sailor **costume** in the school play.

SYNONYM	ANTONYM

WRITING TIME!

Use *costume* in an original sentence of your own creation.

_____

_____

_____

_____

_____

_____

_____

_____

_____

misty

mist·y • [mIs-tee]

- adjective

 1. *obscured by or covered with mist or something resembling mist*

The early morning forest air was cool and **misty**.

SYNONYM	ANTONYM

WRITING TIME!

Use *misty* in an original sentence of your own creation.

SECTION TWO: WORD REVIEW

Congratulations on learning eight amazing new words! Remember that the whole point of learning new vocabulary is actually to use it, so let's put your new vocabulary to use.

1. Review the words you've learned. Consider what ideas come to mind when you say the words. How about when you read the definitions?

2. Circle at least **two** of your favorites. You'll get to use these when you write your very own story!

focus ——— verb

1. to pay particular attention to;
2. to adjust the focus of (as the eye or a lens)

trust ——— verb

1. to place confidence in : depend;
2. to rely on the truthfulness or accuracy of

repeat ——— verb

1. to say or state again;
2. to make, do, or perform again

creak ——— verb

1. to make a prolonged grating or squeaking sound

bolt ——— verb

1. to move suddenly (as from surprise or fright);
2. to move rapidly

wicked ——— adjective

1. evil in character, behavior, tendency, or influence

costume ——— noun

1. a set of clothes in a style typical of a particular country, occupation, occasion, or historical period

misty ——— adjective

1. obscured by or covered with mist or something resembling mist

STORY TWO

1. List the words you've chosen:

_____

2. Write a story that incorporates all of your chosen words. If you can't think of anything to write about, consider these suggestions:
   - **Write a story that only includes animals.**
   - **Write a story that begins, "It was the middle of the night."**

Wonderful Words for First Grade Vocabulary & Writing Workbook ©2021 Grammaropolis LLC

Section Three: Word Preview
Welcome to your eight new favorite words!

When you encounter a new word, take a moment to consider what it might mean.

1. Think about the word and circle what part of speech you think it is. (*Many words can act as more than one part of speech, depending on how they're used in the sentence, **so only choose one part of speech below.***)

2. Come up with a brief definition of the word in the part of speech you've chosen. It doesn't have to be the *correct* definition—just do your best.

rescue

Part of Speech: noun   verb   adjective

Definition:_____

_____

dodge

Part of Speech: noun   verb   adjective

Definition:_____

_____

decide

Part of Speech: noun   verb   adjective

Definition:_____

_____

jealous

Part of Speech: noun   verb   adjective

Definition:_____

_____

rapid

Part of Speech: noun   verb   adjective

Definition:_____

_____

glum

Part of Speech: noun   verb   adjective

Definition:_____

_____

dart

Part of Speech: noun   verb   adjective

Definition:_____

_____

grumpy

Part of Speech: noun   verb   adjective

Definition:_____

_____

rescue

res·cue　•　[rE-skyoo]

- verb

　1. to free from confinement, violence, danger, or evil

We **rescued** our puppy from the city pound.

SYNONYM	ANTONYM

WRITING TIME!

Use *rescue* in an original sentence of your own creation.

---

dodge

dodge • [dAHj]

- verb

1. to behave evasively in speech or action

Gerald threw a ball at me, but I **dodged** it.

SYNONYM	ANTONYM

WRITING TIME!

Use *dodge* in an original sentence of your own creation.

decide

de·cide • [di-sIEd]

- verb

> 1. to arrive at a choice or solution that ends uncertainty or contention

Please **decide** if you want the grilled cheese or the burger.

SYNONYM	ANTONYM

WRITING TIME!
Use *decide* in an original sentence of your own creation.

jealous

jeal·ous • [jEl-uhs]

- **adjective**
  1. *feeling or showing envy of someone or their achievements and advantages*

  My little brother is **jealous** because I got a new bicycle.

Synonym

_____
_____
_____

Antonym

_____
_____
_____

Writing Time!
Use *jealous* in an original sentence of your own creation.

rapid

rap·id • [rAp-uhd]

- adjective

1. marked by a notably high rate of motion, or activity: requiring notably little time

The **rapid** water swept my shoes away almost instantly.

SYNONYM	ANTONYM

WRITING TIME!

Use *rapid* in an original sentence of your own creation.

_____

_____

_____

_____

_____

_____

_____

_____

_____

glum

glum • [glUHm]

- adjective
  1. looking or feeling dejected

My mom was feeling **glum** because her favorite team lost.

SYNONYM	ANTONYM

WRITING TIME!
Use *glum* in an original sentence of your own creation.

dart

dart • [dAHRt]

- **verb**

1. to thrust or move with sudden speed

The fish **darted** away before I could catch it with my net.

Synonym	Antonym
_____	_____
_____	_____

Writing Time!

Use *dart* in an original sentence of your own creation.

_____

_____

_____

_____

_____

_____

grumpy

grump·y • [grUHm-pee]

- adjective

1. moodily cross: surly, ill-humored

Why are you in such a **grumpy** mood today?

SYNONYM	ANTONYM

WRITING TIME!

Use *grumpy* in an original sentence of your own creation.

SECTION THREE: WORD REVIEW

Congratulations on learning eight amazing new words! Remember that the whole point of learning new vocabulary is actually to use it, so let's put your new vocabulary to use.

1. Review the words you've learned. Consider what ideas come to mind when you say the words. How about when you read the definitions?

2. Circle at least **two** of your favorites. You'll get to use these when you write your very own story!

rescue —— verb
1. to free from confinement, violence, danger, or evil

dodge —— verb
1. to behave evasively in speech or action

decide —— verb
1. to arrive at a choice or solution that ends uncertainty or contention

jealous —— adjective
1. feeling or showing envy of someone or their achievements and advantages

rapid —— adjective
1. marked by a notably high rate of motion, or activity: requiring notably little time

glum —— adjective
1. looking or feeling dejected

dart —— verb
1. to thrust or move with sudden speed

grumpy —— adjective
1. moodily cross: surly, ill-humored

STORY THREE

1. List the words you've chosen:

_____

2. Write a story that incorporates all of your chosen words. If you can't think of anything to write about, consider these suggestions:
   - **Write a story that takes place in your school.**
   - **Write a story that takes place in outer space.**

_____

_____
_____

_____
_____

_____
_____

_____
_____

_____
_____

SECTION FOUR: WORD PREVIEW
Welcome to your eight new favorite words!

When you encounter a new word, take a moment to consider what it might mean.

1. Think about the word and circle what part of speech you think it is.
   *(Many words can act as more than one part of speech, depending on how they're used in the sentence, **so only choose one part of speech below**.)*

2. Come up with a brief definition of the word in the part of speech you've chosen. It doesn't have to be the *correct* definition—just do your best.

ticket
Part of Speech: noun   verb   adjective

Definition:_____

_____

sly
Part of Speech: noun   verb   adjective

Definition:_____

_____

blink
Part of Speech: noun   verb   adjective

Definition:_____

_____

cozy
Part of Speech: noun   verb   adjective

Definition:_____

_____

ache
Part of Speech: noun   verb   adjective

Definition:_____

_____

wonder
Part of Speech: noun   verb   adjective

Definition:_____

_____

equal
Part of Speech: noun   verb   adjective

Definition:_____

_____

cue
Part of Speech: noun   verb   adjective

Definition:_____

_____

ticket

tick·et • [tIk-uht]

- noun

1. a piece of paper or small card that gives the holder a certain right

We need a **ticket** in order to get on the airplane.

SYNONYM	ANTONYM

WRITING TIME!

Use *ticket* in an original sentence of your own creation.

sly

sly • [slIE]

- **adjective**
    1. artfully cunning;
    2. lightly artful or mischievous

That **sly** con artist tried to trick me!

SYNONYM	ANTONYM

WRITING TIME!
Use *sly* in an original sentence of your own creation.

blink

blink • [blINGk]

- verb
1. *to shut and open the eyes quickly;*
2. *to shine intermittently: flicker, twinkle*

The hall light **blinked** on and off all night, so I hardly slept.

SYNONYM	ANTONYM

WRITING TIME!
Use *blink* in an original sentence of your own creation.

cozy

co·zy • [kOH-zee]

> **- adjective**
> *1. giving a feeling of comfort, warmth, and relaxation*
>
> My little sister's bed is really **cozy** and I love to lie in it.

SYNONYM	ANTONYM

WRITING TIME!
Use *cozy* in an original sentence of your own creation.

ache

ache • [AYk]

- noun
1. *a dull persistent pain;*
2. *a condition marked by aching*

I have a stomach **ache** after eating all of that chocolate pie.

SYNONYM	ANTONYM

WRITING TIME!
Use *ache* in an original sentence of your own creation.

wonder

won·der   •   [wUHn-duhr]

- verb
1. *to wish to know something;*
2. *to be in a state of rapt attention*

I **wonder** why Caroline didn't invite me to her party.

SYNONYM	ANTONYM

WRITING TIME!

Use *wonder* in an original sentence of your own creation.

equal

e·qual • [EE-kwuhl]

- adjective

1. of the same measure, quantity, amount, regard, or number as another or others

Make sure the twins get **equal** portions of ice cream.

SYNONYM	ANTONYM

WRITING TIME!

Use *equal* in an original sentence of your own creation.

_____

_____

_____

_____

_____

_____

_____

_____

_____

_____

cue

cue • [kyOO]

- noun

1. a signal (such as a word, phrase, or movement) to begin a specific speech or action

My brothers' loud yelling was my **cue** to leave the house.

SYNONYM

ANTONYM

WRITING TIME!

Use *cue* in an original sentence of your own creation.

Section Four: Word Review

Congratulations on learning eight amazing new words! Remember that the whole point of learning new vocabulary is actually to use it, so let's put your new vocabulary to use.

1. Review the words you've learned. Consider what ideas come to mind when you say the words. How about when you read the definitions?
2. Circle at least **two** of your favorites. You'll get to use these when you write your very own story!

ticket ———— noun
1. *a piece of paper or small card that gives the holder a certain right*

sly ———— adjective
1. *artfully cunning;*
2. *lightly artful or mischievous*

blink ———— verb
1. *to shut and open the eyes quickly;*
2. *to shine intermittently: flicker, twinkle*

cozy ———— adjective
1. *giving a feeling of comfort, warmth, and relaxation*

ache ———— noun
1. *a dull persistent pain;*
2. *a condition marked by aching*

wonder ———— verb
1. *to wish to know something;*
2. *to be in a state of rapt attention*

equal ———— adjective
1. *of the same measure, quantity, amount, regard, or number as another or others*

cue ———— noun
1. *a signal (such as a word, phrase, or movement) to begin a specific speech or action*

STORY FOUR

1. List the words you've chosen:

_____

2. Write a story that incorporates all of your chosen words. If you can't
   think of anything to write about, consider these suggestions:
   - **Write a story that features a magician.**
   - **Write a story in which the main character has a superpower.**

_____

_____
_____

_____
_____

_____
_____

_____
_____

SECTION FIVE: WORD PREVIEW
Welcome to your eight new favorite words!

When you encounter a new word, take a moment to consider what it might mean.

1. Think about the word and circle what part of speech you think it is. *(Many words can act as more than one part of speech, depending on how they're used in the sentence, **so only choose one part of speech below.**)*

2. Come up with a brief definition of the word in the part of speech you've chosen. It doesn't have to be the *correct* definition—just do your best.

belong
Part of Speech: noun   verb   adjective

*Definition:*_____

gigantic
Part of Speech: noun   verb   adjective

*Definition:*_____

attach
Part of Speech: noun   verb   adjective

*Definition:*_____

rusty
Part of Speech: noun   verb   adjective

*Definition:*_____

seed
Part of Speech: noun   verb   adjective

*Definition:*_____

deserve
Part of Speech: noun   verb   adjective

*Definition:*_____

timid
Part of Speech: noun   verb   adjective

*Definition:*_____

cave
Part of Speech: noun   verb   adjective

*Definition:*_____

belong

be·long • [bee-lOHng]

> **- verb**
>   *1. to be the property of a person or thing*
>   *2. to be a member or part of a particular group*
>
> Those shoes aren't yours; they **belong** to Sandra.

SYNONYM

ANTONYM

WRITING TIME!
Use *belong* in an original sentence of your own creation.

gigantic

gi·gan·tic • [jie-gAn-tik]

> **- adjective**
> *1. of very great size or extent: huge or enormous.*
>
> Katy ordered a **gigantic** ice cream sundae, and of course she couldn't finish it all.

SYNONYM	ANTONYM

WRITING TIME!
Use *gigantic* in an original sentence of your own creation.

_____

_____

_____

_____

_____

_____

_____

_____

_____

_____

_____

attach

at·tach • [uh-tAch]

- verb

  1. to fasten or join

Be sure you **attach** your water bottle to the outside of your backpack.

SYNONYM	ANTONYM

WRITING TIME!

Use *attach* in an original sentence of your own creation.

rusty

rust·y • [rUHs-tee]

- **adjective**
  1. *affected by or coated with rust;*
  2. *(of a skill) impaired through lack of practice or old age*

We left the scissors outside all month, and they got all **rusty**.

SYNONYM	ANTONYM

WRITING TIME!
Use *rusty* in an original sentence of your own creation.

_____

_____

_____

_____

_____

_____

_____

seed

seed • [sEEd]

- noun

1. something that is planted or can be planted

Bury the orange **seed** in the backyard, and someday an orange tree might grow from it.

SYNONYM	ANTONYM

WRITING TIME!

Use *seed* in an original sentence of your own creation.

deserve

de·serve • [di-zUHRv]

- verb
1. *to come to be rightfully worthy of;*
2. *to be rightfully qualified to have or receive*

Laurence worked hard on her project, so she **deserved** an "A."

SYNONYM

ANTONYM

WRITING TIME!

Use *deserve* in an original sentence of your own creation.

timid

tim·id • [tIm-uhd]

- adjective
> *1. lacking in courage or self confidence*

If I weren't so **timid**, I would try out for the field hockey team.

SYNONYM	ANTONYM
_____	_____
_____	_____

WRITING TIME!
Use *timid* in an original sentence of your own creation.

_____

_____
_____

_____

_____

_____

_____

_____

_____

_____

cave

cave • [kAYv]

- **noun**

1. a hollowed-out chamber in the earth or in the side of a cliff or hill

The hikers found an old **cave** for shelter during the storm.

SYNONYM	ANTONYM

WRITING TIME!

Use *cave* in an original sentence of your own creation.

SECTION FIVE: WORD REVIEW

Congratulations on learning eight amazing new words! Remember that the whole point of learning new vocabulary is actually to use it, so let's put your new vocabulary to use.

1. Review the words you've learned. Consider what ideas come to mind when you say the words. How about when you read the definitions?
2. Circle at least **two** of your favorites. You'll get to use these when you write your very own story!

belong ———— verb
1. to be the property of a person or thing
2. to be a member or part of a particular group

gigantic ———— adjective
1. of very great size or extent: huge or enormous.

attach ———— verb
1. to fasten or join

rusty ———— adjective
1. affected by or coated with rust;
2. (of a skill) impaired through lack of practice or old age

seed ———— noun
1. something that is planted or can be planted

deserve ———— verb
1. to come to be rightfully worthy of;
2. to be rightfully qualified to have or receive

timid ———— adjective
1. lacking in courage or self confidence

cave ———— noun
1. a hollowed-out chamber in the earth or in the side of a cliff or hill

STORY FIVE

1. List the words you've chosen:

_____

_____

2. Write a story that incorporates all of your chosen words. If you can't think of anything to write about, consider these suggestions:
   - **Write a story that includes your favorite dessert.**
   - **Write a story that starts, "Once upon a time, there was a sad sea lion."**

_____

_____
_____

_____
_____

_____
_____

_____
_____

Wonderful Words for First Grade Vocabulary & Writing Workbook ©2021 Grammaropolis LLC

Wonderful Words for First Grade Vocabulary & Writing Workbook ©2021 Grammaropolis LLC

SECTION SIX: WORD PREVIEW
Welcome to your eight new favorite words!

When you encounter a new word, take a moment to consider what it might mean.

1. Think about the word and circle what part of speech you think it is.
   *(Many words can act as more than one part of speech, depending on how they're used in the sentence, **so only choose one part of speech below**.)*
2. Come up with a brief definition of the word in the part of speech you've chosen. It doesn't have to be the *correct* definition—just do your best.

filthy
Part of Speech: noun   verb   adjective

Definition:_____

_____

batch
Part of Speech: noun   verb   adjective

Definition:_____

_____

prefer
Part of Speech: noun   verb   adjective

Definition:_____

_____

forest
Part of Speech: noun   verb   adjective

Definition:_____

_____

sprinkle
Part of Speech: noun   verb   adjective

Definition:_____

_____

leader
Part of Speech: noun   verb   adjective

Definition:_____

_____

fasten
Part of Speech: noun   verb   adjective

Definition:_____

_____

chimney
Part of Speech: noun   verb   adjective

Definition:_____

_____

filthy

fil·thy • [fil-thee]

- adjective
  1. *covered with, having the appearance of, or containing filth;*
  2. *disgustingly dirty*

My shoes were **filthy** after I walked through the mud.

SYNONYM	ANTONYM

WRITING TIME!
Use *filthy* in an original sentence of your own creation.

batch

batch • [baCH]

- noun

1. the quantity of goods or material produced at one time

The first **batch** of cookies is always the hardest to bake.

SYNONYM	ANTONYM

WRITING TIME!

Use *batch* in an original sentence of your own creation.

prefer

pre·fer • [pri-fUHR]

> **- verb**
> *1. to have a preference for*
>
> My little cousin **prefers** jelly beans instead of milk chocolate.

SYNONYM	ANTONYM

WRITING TIME!

Use *prefer* in an original sentence of your own creation.

_____

_____

_____

_____

_____

_____

_____

_____

_____

_____

forest

for·est • [fOR-uhst]

- noun

   1. *a dense growth of trees and underbrush covering a large tract of land*

We like to go hiking through the **forest** in the mountains.

SYNONYM	ANTONYM
_____	_____
_____	_____

WRITING TIME!

Use *forest* in an original sentence of your own creation.

sprinkle

sprin·kle • [sprING-kuhl]

- verb
  1. to scatter in drops or particles

When the cake was done, I **sprinkled** bits of cookie on top.

SYNONYM	ANTONYM

WRITING TIME!
Use *sprinkle* in an original sentence of your own creation.

leader

lead·er • [IEE-duhr]

- noun

1. a person or animal that leads

We have to follow the **leader** on the hike, or we will get lost!

SYNONYM	ANTONYM

WRITING TIME!

Use *leader* in an original sentence of your own creation.

fasten

fas·ten • [fAss-in]

- verb
    1. *to close or do up securely*
    2. *to make firm or strong*

Please **fasten** your seat belts before we start the car.

SYNONYM	ANTONYM

WRITING TIME!

Use *fasten* in an original sentence of your own creation.

chimney

chim·ney • [chIM-nee]

- noun

1. a vertical channel or structure that carries off smoke or other undesirable fumes or gases

Our **chimney** was clogged, so the room filled up with smoke!

SYNONYM	ANTONYM

WRITING TIME!

Use *chimney* in an original sentence of your own creation.

Section Six: Word Review

Congratulations on learning eight amazing new words! Remember that the whole point of learning new vocabulary is actually to use it, so let's put your new vocabulary to use.

1. Review the words you've learned. Consider what ideas come to mind when you say the words. How about when you read the definitions?

2. Circle at least **two** of your favorites. You'll get to use these when you write your very own story!

filthy — adjective
1. *covered with, having the appearance of, or containing filth*
2. *disgustingly dirty*

batch — noun
1. *the quantity of goods or material produced at one time*

prefer — verb
1. *to have a preference for*

forest — noun
1. *a dense growth of trees and underbrush covering a large tract of land*

sprinkle — verb
1. *to scatter in drops or particles*

leader — noun
1. *a person or animal that leads*

fasten — verb
1. *to close or do up securely;*
2. *to make firm or strong*

chimney — noun
1. *a vertical channel or structure that carries off smoke or other undesirable fumes or gases*

STORY SIX

1. List the words you've chosen:

_____

2. Write a story that incorporates all of your chosen words. If you can't think of anything to write about, consider these suggestions:
   - **Write a story in which your main character is your parent or guardian.**
   - **Write a story that starts, "Bananas don't taste like cheese."**

_____
_____
_____
_____
_____
_____
_____
_____
_____
_____
_____
_____
_____
_____

Wonderful Words for First Grade Vocabulary & Writing Workbook ©2021 Grammaropolis LLC

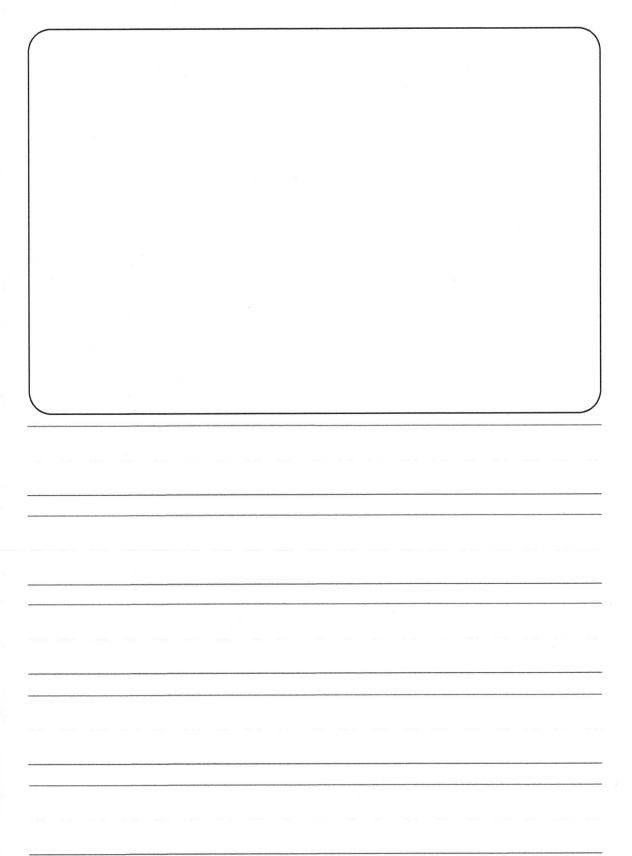

INDEX OF WORDS USED

ache	56	focus	24
alone	16	forest	83
attach	68	gigantic	67
basket	10	glum	43
batch	81	grumpy	45
belong	66	ignore	13
blink	54	jealous	41
bolt	28	leader	85
bundle	14	misty	31
cave	73	narrow	17
chat	11	nibble	15
chimney	87	prefer	82
costume	30	rapid	42
cozy	55	repeat	26
crash	12	rescue	38
creak	27	rusty	69
cue	59	seed	70
dart	44	sly	53
decide	40	sprinkle	84
deserve	71	ticket	52
dodge	39	timid	72
equal	58	trust	25
fasten	86	wicked	29
filthy	80	wonder	57